DISCOVERING Space

THE SUN

Ian Graham

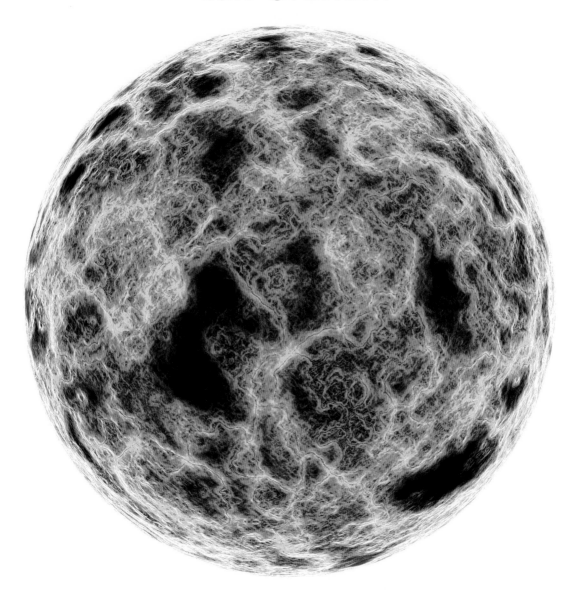

A+

Smart Apple Media

Published by Smart Apple Media
2140 Howard Drive West
North Mankato, MN 56003

Created by Q2A Creative
Series Editor: Honor Head
Designers: Diksha Khatri, Ashita Murgai
Picture Researchers: Lalit Dalal, Jyoti Sachdev

Picture credits
t=top, b=bottom l=left, r=right, m=middle
Cover images: Courtesy of Science Photo Library / Photolibrary
Nasa: 4b, 21m, Winfried Wisniewski/ zefa Corbis: 4-5 (background), NOAA /Grant W. Goodge: 5t, ESA: 6–7b, 20b,
Bettmann/Corbis: 8b, Science Photo Library/ Photolibrary: 10t, 15t, 15b, 17t, 19t, 20-21m(Background), 23b, 26b,
Peter Elvidge/ Istockphoto: 11b, Nasa/MODIS/ USGS: 12b, Bryan F. Peterson/ Corbis: 13(background), SOHO (ESA & Nasa):
14b, 23t, Nasa, The Hubble Heritage Team, STScI, AURA & HEIC: 16b. 16-17 (background), Nasa/ JPL: 18m, Roman Krochuk/
Istockphoto: 18-19(background), Copyright 1980 by Fred Espenak,www.MrEclipse.com: 22t, NOAO/AURA/NSF: 22b,
Paul Morley/ Shutterstock: 24, Roger Ressmeyer/Corbis: 25, A. Dupree (CfA), R. Gilliland (STScI), NASA: 27t.

Printed in China

Library of Congress Cataloging-in-Publication Data

Graham, Ian, 1953–
The sun / by Ian Graham.
p. cm. — (Discovering space)
Includes index.
ISBN 978-1-59920-069-9
1. Sun—Juvenile literature. I. Title.

QB521.5.G723 2007
523.7—dc22   2006100029

First Edition

9 8 7 6 5 4 3 2 1

Contents

The sun

Without the sun, Earth would be a dry, cold, brown, lifeless rock. The sun provides light and heat, which most living things need to survive. It warms the land and sea and makes moisture **evaporate** from the oceans, lakes, and rivers to form rain clouds.

Our solar system

The sun is in the middle of a group of eight **planets**. The planets travel around the sun. The paths they follow around the sun are called orbits. The sun, the planets, their **moons,** and everything else orbiting the sun are called the **solar system.**

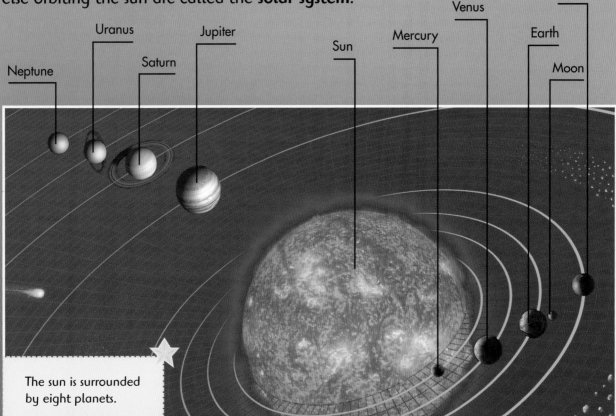

Neptune — Uranus — Saturn — Jupiter — Sun — Mercury — Venus — Earth — Mars — Moon

The sun is surrounded by eight planets.

The sun sets in the west, lighting up the clouds in that direction.

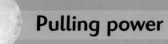

Pulling power

Earth's **gravity** pulls things to the ground. The sun has gravity, too, which holds the planets in their orbits. Without the sun's gravity, the planets would fly off into deep space and the solar system would not exist.

Spotlight on
space

The sun is the biggest object in the solar system. It is more than a million times bigger than Earth. The sun is so big that it contains 500 times more matter than everything else in the solar system put together.

WARNING!
Never look straight at the sun and never look at it through a camera, binoculars, or a telescope. The light from the sun is so strong that it can make you blind, even if you are wearing dark glasses.

Our star

The sun is a **star**, just like the many thousands of other stars in the sky. It looks bigger and brighter than all of the other stars because it is closer to Earth. The sun is our star. It is the only star in Earth's solar system.

Inside the sun

The *SOHO* **space probe** has been finding out what happens inside the sun by studying waves that spread across the sun, like ripples on a pond. These ripples give clues to what is happening inside the sun.

SOHO mission

Launched	▶	December 2, 1995
Orbit	▶	932,000 miles (1.5 million km) away from Earth facing the sun
Size	▶	31 feet (9.5 m) across its solar panels
Weight	▶	4,078 pounds (1,850 kg)

Sun facts

Size across the middle	▶	864,948 miles (1,392,000 km)
Mass	▶	as much as 333,000 Earths
Distance from Earth	▶	about 93 million miles (150 million km)

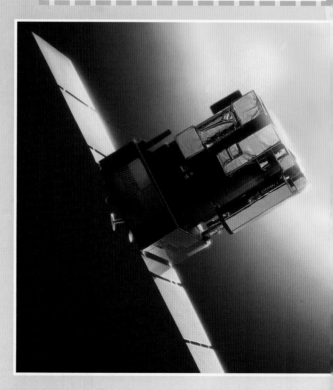

Spotlight on
space

It is hard to understand how far away the sun is from Earth. The fastest way to travel on Earth is by jet plane. If a jetplane could fly from Earth to the sun, it would take nearly 19 years to get there.

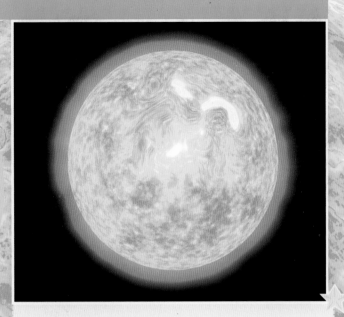

The *SOHO* space probe takes close-up pictures of the sun and sends them to scientists on Earth.

The sun is yellow because of its temperature. Hotter stars are blue or white. Cooler stars are red.

The giant sun

The sun looks like a small ball in the sky, but it is a giant compared to Earth. It is as wide as 109 Earths placed side by side. If there was a bag the size of the sun, it would take more than one million Earths to fill it. And if the sun could be placed on one end of a seesaw, it would take 333,000 Earths on the other end to balance it.

The *SOHO* spacecraft uses 12 instruments to constantly watch the sun.

Myth and magic

People in ancient civilizations had some strange beliefs to explain the rising and setting of the sun and its movement across the sky. They created stories to explain what they saw. One common idea was that the sun rode across the sky in a chariot or boat.

Sky chariot

The sun god of ancient Greece was named Helios. Every day, Helios crossed the sky from east to west in a fiery chariot pulled by horses. Then he had to get back to the east for the next morning. So, during the night, he sailed east on the ocean, out of sight inside a golden cup.

Sun gods

Many ancient civilizations had sun gods.

	Name of sun god
Egyptian	Ra
Greek	Helios
Roman	Sol or Apollo
Hindu	Surya
Inca	Inti
Inuit	Malina

Helios rode across the sky in a glowing chariot pulled by horses. The glowing sun was Helios's fiery crown.

Ancient Egypt

More than 4,000 years ago, the ancient Egyptians worshipped a sun god named Ra. They believed Ra sailed across the sky in a boat during the day. At night, he made his way back through the underworld, ready to set sail across the sky again the next morning. They believed that in the underworld Ra met Apopis, a demon. Every night Apopis fought with Ra, but he could not kill him, so Ra was able to appear in his boat every morning to start a new day.

In ancient Egypt, the sun god Ra was shown with the sun in his headdress.

Spotlight on
space

During winter, the sun does not rise as high in the sky as it does in summer. In some ancient civilizations, people thought this might be because the sun god had become ill and weak.

Telling time

People have used the sun to measure time for thousands of years. The sun's rising and setting mark the beginning and end of each day. The position of the sun in the sky during the day tells us the time of day. As Earth moves around the sun, it creates the four seasons that make a year.

As Earth moves around the sun, half of Earth is in sunlight while the other half is in darkness.

Calendar facts

Every fourth year, one extra day is added to the end of February to make the calendar catch up with the sun. The year with the extra day is called a leap year.

Length of a solar day	▶ 24 hours
Length of a solar year	▶ 365.24 days
Length of a calendar year	▶ 365 days

Day and night

The sun does not really move across the sky—it is Earth that is always moving. Earth is constantly spinning. When you are on the side of Earth that faces the sun, it is daytime. Then Earth spins around until you are on the side that faces away from the sun—this is when nighttime begins.

Winter in the northern hemisphere and summer in the southern hemisphere

Earth

Sun

Summer in the northern hemisphere and winter in the southern hemisphere

The seasons are caused by Earth's tilt. When it is summer in the north, it is winter in the south.

Spotlight on
space

When the North Pole is tilted toward the sun, the sun does not set there for six months. This means there is no day or night—it is light all the time. When it is daylight at the North Pole, it is dark at the South Pole.

Earth's seasons

Earth **tilts** like a spinning top leaning over. As Earth moves around the sun, it tilts toward the sun for part of the year, then tilts away from the sun for the rest of the year. The weather is warmer when Earth tilts toward the sun and cooler when it tilts away from the sun. This produces the changing seasons.

A **sundial** uses shadows to tell the time. As the sun's position changes in the sky, the shadows on the sundial show what time it is.

Life-giver

Four things are needed for life on Earth—light, warmth, oxygen, and water. The sun provides light and warmth, which make green plants grow. Green plants make oxygen. The heat from the sun causes evaporation which produces rain. This means that Earth has a constant supply of water.

Life on Earth

If Earth was a lot closer to the sun, all of its water would have boiled away long ago. If it was much farther away from the sun, its water would be solid ice. A planet needs to be the right distance from a star for life to develop as it has on Earth. This distance is called the **life zone**.

Sunshine and water make life possible. Most of Earth is covered by water.

Life zone

A planet needs to be a certain distance from a star for life to survive.

Closest	▶	75 million miles (120 million km)
Farthest	▶	150 million miles (240 million km)
Distance of Earth from the sun	▶	93 million miles (150 million km)

Solar energy

Solar energy is the **energy** Earth receives from the sun. Animals need this solar energy to live and grow, but they cannot use energy straight from the sun. They get it by eating green plants or by eating other animals that live on green plants. Green plants take in energy from the sun and use it for growth by a process called **photosynthesis**.

Earth receives just a tiny part of the huge amount of energy given by the sun, but it is enough to support life on Earth.

Spotlight on
space

In only one hour, the sun could supply the world with enough energy for everyone for a year. This would be the same amount of energy that we now get from coal, oil, gas, and nuclear power stations.

Inside the sun

The sun is not solid like Earth. There is no hard ground to walk on, even if people could survive the scorching heat. Scientists cannot see through the sun, but they have still managed to learn what it is like inside.

Heat and light

The heat and light that flow from the sun come from its **core**. Particles of **matter** at the center of the sun are so hot and are pressed together so hard that they stick to each other. This is called **nuclear fusion** and it makes a lot of energy.

Heat and light escape into space

All of the sun's energy is produced at its core.

Energy travels outward

Energy is produced in the sun's core

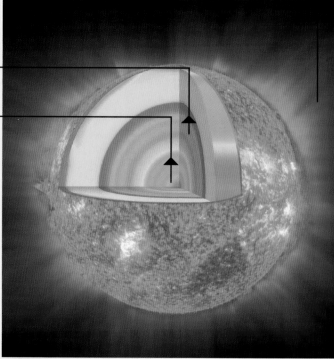

The sun's heat

Temperature at core	60 million °F (16 million °C)
Temperature at surface	9,932 °F (5,500 °C)

Spotlight on
space

The part of the sun that can be seen is the part that gives off light. It is called the photosphere. It is also called the sun's surface, although there is no solid ground. The photosphere is covered by hot gas called the chromosphere. On top of this, there is another layer of even hotter gas called the corona.

It takes hundreds of thousands of years for energy to go from the sun's core to its surface, but it takes only eight minutes to reach Earth.

Boiling gas

Energy flows out in all directions from the sun's core. Gas boils up to the surface, carrying the energy with it. When the energy escapes into space, the gas cools and sinks again. Then more hot gas rises to take its place. This makes the sun's surface look like a pan of boiling water. Each of the bubbles of hot gas on the sun is about 620 miles (998 km) across.

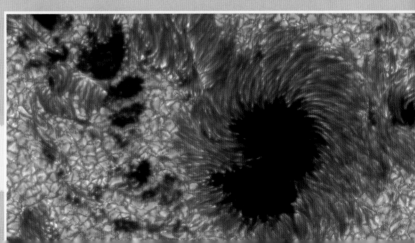

Gas boils up to the surface of the sun around a dark **sunspot**.

The sun's birth

There was a time, long ago, when there was no sun. Instead, there was a giant cloud of gas and dust swirling in space. The sun formed from this cloud about 4.5 billion years ago.

Spinning disk

The cloud began to slowly collapse, like a leaking party balloon. This happened because the cloud's own gravity pulled it inward on itself. Then the whole cloud started spinning and became a flattened disk, like a spinning plate. Gas falling inward made a big ball at the center of the disk, and this became the sun.

A huge cloud of gas and dust like this gave birth to the sun.

A new sun

Cloud collapsed for	▶	up to 1 million years
Sun heated up for	▶	50 million years
At last	▶	the cloud of heated gas became the sun

The sun formed in the middle of a spinning disk of gas and dust.

Switching on

At first, the young sun did not shine—it was just a big ball of gas. As more gas fell onto it, the sun's gravity grew stronger. Gravity pressed the gas at the center harder and harder. The pressing heated the gas, and when it was hot enough, the sun became a dazzling star.

Scientists are trying to build power stations on Earth that work like the sun. It may take another 50 years or more to get the first one working.

Spotlight on
space

The sun shines because it changes matter into heat, light, and other forms of energy. Every second the sun loses about 4.4 million tons (4 million t) of matter. But it still has enough left to keep shining for billions of years.

Wind in space

Particles of matter escape into space from the sun all the time, like steam from boiling water. About 1,102,311 tons (1,000,000 t) of these particles fly out from the sun every second. They go in all directions at great speeds. This is called **solar wind**.

Capsule cover closes over base to protect it during return to Earth

Solar wind collectors

Re-entry capsule

The *Genesis* spacecraft has round dishes that trap solar wind particles.

Solar panel

Genesis

A spacecraft called *Genesis* was sent to collect solar wind particles and bring them back to Earth. The capsule with the particles inside crashed to the ground on Earth instead of landing safely, but solar wind particles were still stored inside the dishes. Scientists are now studying them.

Genesis mission

Launched	▶	August 8, 2001
Collection phase	▶	December 3, 2001 to April 2, 2004
Returned to Earth	▶	September 8, 2004

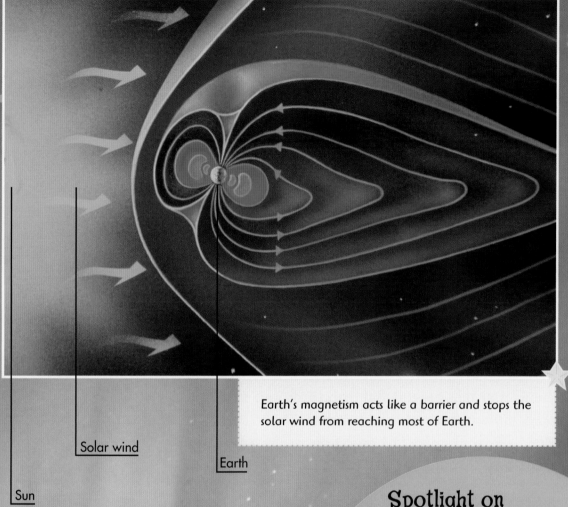

Sun

Solar wind

Earth

Earth's magnetism acts like a barrier and stops the solar wind from reaching most of Earth.

Sky lights

The solar wind travels all the way to Earth and far beyond. Earth acts like a big magnet. Its magnetism pushes the solar wind away from Earth, except at the North and South Poles. When the solar wind hits the air above the Poles, it makes streaks of shimmering colors appear in the sky. This is called an **aurora**.

An aurora lights up the sky as particles of the solar wind crash into air high above the ground.

Spotlight on
space

The solar wind travels amazingly fast. The slowest solar wind particles fly at 124 miles (200 km) per second. The fastest travel at 621 miles (1,000 km) per second. At this speed, you could zoom around the world in 40 seconds.

Sun storms

From Earth, the sun looks like a plain yellow ball. But a closer look would show giant storms raging across the sun. The sun's fiery surface is boiling and there are giant streaks of gas flying out into space.

The *Cluster* mission

The *Cluster* mission sent four **satellites** into space to learn more about the solar wind and how sun storms affect Earth. It is the first time four spacecraft have ever flown through space together.

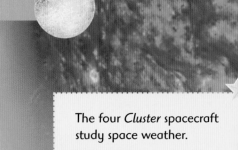

The four *Cluster* spacecraft study space weather.

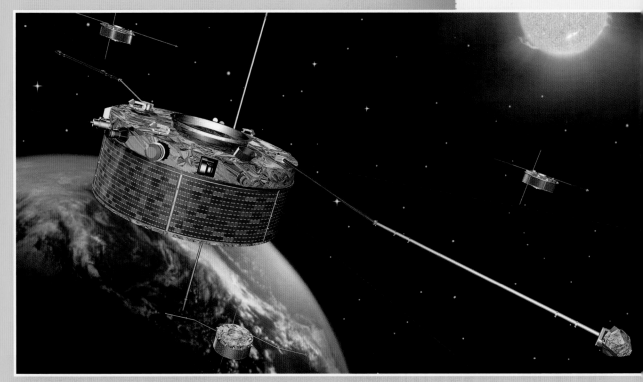

The first *Cluster* satellites were launched in 1996, but the rocket carrying them into space blew up, and the satellites crashed to the ground. Four new satellites were launched four years later. This time they were launched two at a time by two rockets, and the launches were successful.

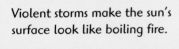
Violent storms make the sun's surface look like boiling fire.

Fountains of gas, bigger than Earth, burst out of the sun's surface.

Cluster mission

Launch of second *Cluster* mission	July 16, 2000 (2 satellites) August 9, 2000 (2 satellites)
Number of satellites	4
Names of satellites	*Rumba* *Salsa* *Samba* *Tango*
Orbit	11,806–73,943 miles (19,000–119,000 km) above Earth

Power cuts

Storms on the sun sometimes fling huge amounts of gas into space. This gas can fly in any direction. If the gas comes toward Earth, it can cause power outages and problems with radios and cell phones. In 1989, a huge sun storm caused power outages in Canada. Scientists study the sun every day, looking for signs of the next big storm that might affect Earth.

Studying the sun

Scientists can study the sun in two ways: they use telescopes on Earth and telescopes in space. Telescopes that study the sun are called solar telescopes. They are specially designed for looking at the sun without being damaged by its intense light and heat.

Solar scope

The McMath-Pierce telescope in the United States is a solar telescope. A mirror at the top of a tall tower reflects the sun down a tunnel. The long tunnel goes underground. More mirrors in the tunnel reflect the sun onto instruments that measure and record every detail.

McMath-Pierce solar telescope

Tower height	▶	33 yards (30.5 m)
Length of tunnel	▶	166 yards (152 m)
Size of sun's image	▶	33 inches (85 cm)
Telescope opened	▶	1962

A mirror reflects light into the tunnel

The McMath-Pierce telescope is the world's biggest solar telescope.

Space telescopes

Some of the energy from the sun cannot go through Earth's **atmosphere**. If this energy does not reach the ground, telescopes on the ground cannot study it. So space scientists are now sending telescopes into space. The telescopes point at the sun and send pictures and measurements back to Earth.

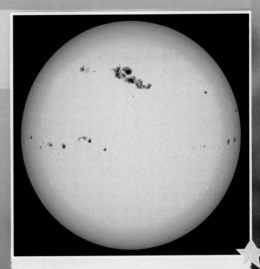

Dark spots, called sunspots, often appear on the sun. Some last a few hours, others last for months.

Spotlight on
space

The sun is magnetic. Sunspots are places where the sun's magnetism becomes very strong for a while. Sunspots look dark because there is dazzling bright gas all around them. If it could be seen by itself, a sunspot would glow orange.

Sunspots have a dark center called the umbra. The umbra has a lighter color around it called the penumbra.

Eclipses

As Earth and the moon move through space, they sometimes line up together with the sun. These special events are called eclipses. When the moon comes between Earth and the sun, it causes a **solar eclipse**.

Size and distance

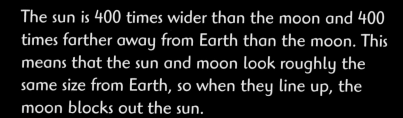

The sun is 400 times wider than the moon and 400 times farther away from Earth than the moon. This means that the sun and moon look roughly the same size from Earth, so when they line up, the moon blocks out the sun.

Spotlight on
space

When the sun is almost covered by the moon, beams of sunlight filter through the edges of the moon. They make a line of bright spots called Baily's Beads, because they look like a string of beads. Sometimes there is just one dazzling spot—it is called a diamond ring, because of the way it sparkles.

The "diamond ring" sparkles during a total eclipse.

Biting the sun

Total eclipses cannot be seen from everywhere on Earth. You can only see a total eclipse from certain places. These places are where the darkest part of the moon's shadow falls during an eclipse. Outside the darkest part of the shadow, the moon covers only part of the sun, and the sun looks as if someone has taken a bite out of it. This is called a partial eclipse.

When the moon covers the sun, the glowing gas around the sun suddenly becomes visible.

Future solar eclipses

Date of eclipse	Will be seen from
August 1, 2008	Arctic Ocean, Siberia, China
July 22, 2009	India, China, South Pacific Ocean
July 11, 2010	South Pacific Ocean
November 13, 2012	Northern Australia, South Pacific Ocean

The future

The sun will not last forever. Two forces are balanced in the sun—gravity and heat. Gravity pulls inward and tries to make the sun smaller. The sun's heat pushes back and tries to make it bigger. If the sun ever cools down, gravity will make the sun collapse in on itself.

The dying sun

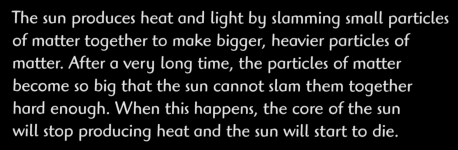

The sun produces heat and light by slamming small particles of matter together to make bigger, heavier particles of matter. After a very long time, the particles of matter become so big that the sun cannot slam them together hard enough. When this happens, the core of the sun will stop producing heat and the sun will start to die.

The sun's life cycle

Formed	▶	4.5 billion years ago
Shines for	▶	nearly 10 billion years
Will die	▶	about 5 billion years from now

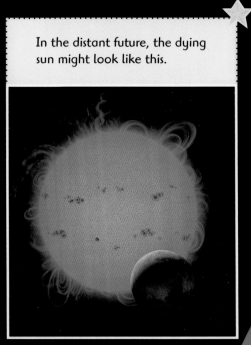

In the distant future, the dying sun might look like this.

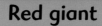

Red giant

When the sun stops making heat, its core will cool down and gravity will pull the sun inward on itself. As the core gets smaller, the outer layers of the sun will swell up and cool. The cooling gas will change from bright yellow to red as the sun dies. The huge dying sun will become a **red giant**. Finally, the gas around the outside of the sun will drift away into space. A tiny star called a **white dwarf** will be left behind.

Betelgeuse is a red giant more than 500 times wider than the sun. It is so big that it is called a supergiant.

Spotlight on
space

What will happen to Earth when the sun dies? As the sun dies, Earth will get hotter and hotter. Life on Earth will become impossible. Eventually, Earth will fall into the sun and burn up. Scientists say that this is likely to happen in about five billion years.

The sun will shine for billions of years before it starts to fade away.

Time line

4.5 billion years ago
The sun is formed from a cloud of gas and dust.

1223 B.C.
A solar eclipse is recorded on a piece of clay.

800 B.C.
A Chinese book, called the *Book of Changes*, includes a description of a sunspot.

270 B.C.
The Greek astronomer Aristarchus of Samos says the sun is at the center of the solar system, but no one believes him.

A.D. 140
The Egyptian astronomer Ptolemy says that Earth is at the center of the solar system, and everyone believes him.

1543
The Polish astronomer Nicolaus Copernicus writes a book that describes the solar system with the sun at its center.

1610
Thomas Harriot, an English mathematician, is the first person to study sunspots with a telescope.

1611
The Italian astronomer Galileo Galilei sees sunspots on the sun.

1633
Galileo says that Copernicus was right and the sun is at the center of the solar system. Galileo is later forced to reject the idea by the Roman Catholic Church.

1668
English astronomer Isaac Newton makes the first reflecting telescope.

1727
Swedish astronomer Anders Celsius and Englishman George Graham see a magnetic storm on the sun.

1754
Englishman John Dollond invents an instrument called a heliometer and uses it to measure the width of the sun.

1769
In Tahiti, an island in the Pacific Ocean, English explorer Captain Cook sees the planet Venus crossing in front of the sun.

1800
English astronomer William Herschel discovers that the sun gives out invisible infrared (heat) rays.

1801
English scientist William Wollaston spreads out sunlight into all of its colors and sees dark lines in the colors.

1815
German scientist Joseph von Fraunhofer does the same experiment as Wollaston. He finds the same dark lines in the rainbow of colors in sunlight. Later, these dark lines help scientists to find out what the sun is made of.

1845
The first photographs of the sun are taken.

1851
The first photograph of a total solar eclipse is taken.

1870
The first photograph of a sun storm, called a prominence, is taken.

1938
Scientists figure out why the sun shines.

1942
Scientists discover that the sun gives out radio waves.

1958
American scientist Eugene Parker thinks there is a solar wind of particles blowing through space from the sun. Few scientists agree with him. They think space is empty.

1959
The Russian space probe *Luna 1* discovers the solar wind.

1962
The McMath-Pierce solar telescope begins observations of the sun.

1973
Astronauts on board the U.S. space station *Skylab* begin studying the sun and filming it from space.

1980
The *Solar Maximum Mission* satellite is launched to study the sun when it is especially stormy.

1989
Storms on the sun cause power outages lasting five hours in Canada.

1990
The *Ulysses* space probe is launched to study the sun by flying over its poles.

1992
After more than 350 years, the Roman Catholic church accepts that Galileo was right when he said that the sun is at the center of the solar system.

1995
The *SOHO* solar space probe is launched.

1996
The four satellites of the *Cluster* mission are destroyed when their *Ariane 5* rocket explodes.

1998
The *TRACE* space probe is launched to observe the sun.

2000
Four new *Cluster* mission satellites are launched by two Russian rockets.

2001
The *Genesis* space probe is launched from the U.S. to collect particles of the solar wind and bring them back to Earth.

2004
The *Genesis* space probe brings particles of the solar wind back to Earth but crashes into the ground.

5 billion years from now
The sun will swell up into a red giant and then shrink to become a white dwarf star.

Glossary

atmosphere The gases that surround most planets, some moons, and stars.

aurora Streaks of different colored lights seen in the sky, especially at the North Pole and South Pole.

calendar year A time period of 12 calendar months lasting 365 days, or 366 days in a leap year.

core The center of a planet or star.

energy We need energy to live. There are many forms of energy, including heat and light.

evaporate Turn from water into vapor when heated by the sun. The water rises into the air, where it forms rain clouds.

gravity An invisible force that pulls things toward each other. Earth's gravity pulls us down to the ground. The sun's gravity keeps Earth and other planets going around the sun.

Inuit Another name for Eskimos, especially those from Greenland and Canada.

life zone The distance a planet must be from a star for life to have a chance of developing.

mass Something that all matter has. The more mass something has, the heavier it is.

matter The particles that gases, liquids, and solid objects are made of.

moons Small objects that orbit a planet. Earth has one moon.

nuclear fusion The process inside the sun that produces energy by smashing small particles of matter together to make bigger particles.

photosynthesis The process plants use to turn sunlight into food.

planets Large, round objects in orbit around a star.

power stations Large buildings used to produce electricity.

red giant A star that has swollen up and turned red near the end of its life.

satellites Moons in orbit around a planet, or spacecraft in orbit around a planet or moon.

SOHO Solar and Heliospheric Observatory.

solar eclipse An event that happens when the moon passes between the sun and Earth.

solar energy Heat, light, and other energy given out by the sun.

solar system The sun, planets, moons, and everything else that orbits the sun.

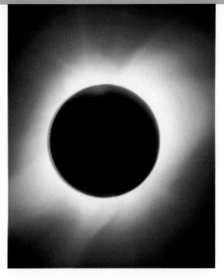

solar wind Particles that fly out of the sun into space in all directions.

solar year The time Earth takes to go around the sun once.

space probe An unmanned spacecraft sent from Earth to explore space.

star Huge, glowing ball of gas. The sun is a star.

sundial An instrument for telling time using a shadow cast by the sun.

sunspot A dark mark that appears on the sun.

tilts Leans to one side slightly.

white dwarf A tiny star, only about as big as Earth, formed when a star such as the sun comes to the end of its life.

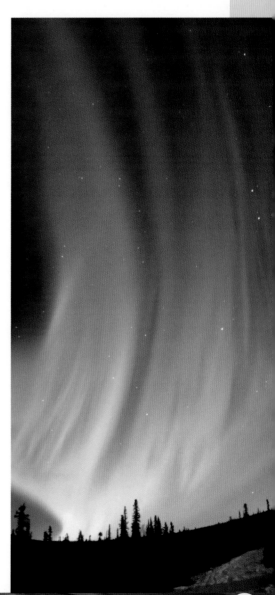

Index

WEB SITES

http://www.frontiernet.net/~kidpower/sun.html

http://www.nasa.gov/vision/universe/solarsystem/sun_for_kids_main.html

http://observe.arc.nasa.gov/nasa/exhibits/sun/sunframe.html

http://starchild.gsfc.nasa.gov/docs/StarChild/solar_system_level1/sun.html

http://www.nationalgeographic.com/solarsystem/ax/low.html?2d

www.kidsastronomy.com/our_sun.htm

http://www.astronomytoday.com/astronomy/sun.html

http://www.noao.edu/image_gallery/solar.html